I0415517

The Unofficial Guide

to the

Military Memorial Ceremony

Chaplain Richard Sones

Copyright © 2013 Richard Sones

All rights reserved.

ISBN-10: 1493790048
ISBN-13: 978-1493790043

To America's Warriors -
Who put their lives on the line daily and too
often make the ultimate sacrifice in defense
of their country.

CONTENTS

INTRODUCTION

As a brand new chaplain on a major Army post, my name came up on the roster for funeral duty. My assigned funeral was to take place two days later at a national cemetery which was nearly two hours from post by staff car. It was, of course, my first military funeral other than having seen brief glimpses in the movies and on television.

I had all kinds of questions about the process, where to stand, when to salute, and so forth. My Brigade chaplain had the same advice for me that the operations officer in my battalion offered; "Just watch the Casualty Affairs Officer, and do what he does."

On the morning of the funeral, I picked up the Casualty Affairs Officer on the way to the cemetery and discovered that this was his first military funeral as well. His comrades told him not to worry, just watch the chaplain, and do what he does.

Fortunately for both of us, I had done some research on the subject and had at least head knowledge of what to do.

The goal of this guide is to offer a resource for chaplains and others who may be responsible for a military memorial ceremony. The first one is always approached with trepidation, and I hope this will put some of that to rest.

This book addresses the "where do I stand?", "what is the process?" questions, not from the approach that says this is the way it must be done, but as a body of possibilities gained from nearly thirty years' experience as a military chaplain. It is detailed enough that a separate company in combat without access to a chaplain can perform a decent memorial ceremony.

There are many individuals in the Army only interested in checking the block; meeting the minimum requirement. A memorial ceremony can be conducted in such a way that it does just that.

I submit that the ceremony can be much more. It is an appropriate time to be moved and inspired in such a way to make the experience unforgettable.

It is my hope that the following pages will instruct, motivate, and encourage those who find themselves in the unenviable position of having to conduct a memorial ceremony so that they will produce a work of art worthy of the price paid by the soldier they endeavor to honor.

The sample messages included at the end of the book are texts from actual military memorial ceremony tributes honoring soldiers killed in combat in Iraq. Their names have been removed from this text, but I will remember them as long as I live.

1 PURPOSE AND INTENT OF THE CEREMONY

A military memorial ceremony should allow the members of a military unit the opportunity to say goodbye to their fallen comrade. It should be conducted in a way that helps bring closure to the event or events that brought about the loss. While the families of fallen soldiers are often invited to attend when possible, the ceremony is intended for the soldiers in the unit. For that reason, the honor and esteem of the unit is celebrated as well as the honor and deeds of the soldier being memorialized.

There are two types of memorial events recognized by Army doctrine. A memorial ceremony is a military ceremony that may have certain religious elements. A memorial service is a religious service which honors the fallen and usually follows their religious tradition. A memorial ceremony is distinct from a memorial service by its ecumenical tone and inclusive nature.

Normally, either a ceremony or a service is conducted. It is possible, however, for the unit to conduct a ceremony and the soldier's religious group to hold a service. This might happen, for example, in the event of the death of a popular chaplain or a commander who is actively involved in a chapel service.

While some outside the military are aghast that Christian chaplains are forced to accommodate soldiers of other faiths by refraining from praying "In Jesus' Name," and even some chaplains balk at the idea, the concept is grounded in scripture and Christian attitude. For a chaplain to point to his insignia and tell the audience that he is going to pray in his tradition while inviting them to pray in theirs is tantamount to proclaiming that he is going to offend them whether they like it or not. Rationalizing that the audience understands and will not take offense is no excuse, even if true.

Memorial ceremonies are usually made mandatory for the soldiers in the unit to attend; therefore, soldiers of many varied and no faith are almost certainly present. The conduct of the ceremony should take that into account. The effective chaplain will not intentionally alienate or offend any of the soldiers whose needs he is responsible to provide for. Paul set an example as he explained in 1st Corinthians, chapter 9: "For though I be free from all men, yet have I made myself servant unto all, that I might gain the more. And unto the Jews I became as a Jew, that I might gain the Jews; to them that are under the law, as under the law, that I might gain them that are under the law; to them that are without law, as without law, (being not without law to God, but under the law to Christ,) that I might gain them that are without law. To the weak became I as weak, that I might gain the weak: I am made all things to all men, that I might by all means save some. And this I do for the gospel's sake, that I might be partaker thereof with you." Paul, in his humility, approached all men where they were and as they were, whether Christian, Jewish, or outside of faith altogether.

The Army regulation on command directs that every

assigned soldier who dies will receive a memorial event. The regulation allows an exception only for a soldier who is convicted of a serious or capital offense or commits such an offense but escapes conviction due to his death. Even so, the unit commander must make the request for an exception to the first general in the chain of command. The regulation specifically states that a soldiers suicide, in and of itself, does not meet the criteria for an exception.

Here is an example of when the exception applies. Many years ago, during a field exercise in Germany, a disgruntled soldier was qualifying with his M-16 at a firing range. When he finished qualifying, he went back to the control tower with his weapon and turned in his empty magazines. At that point, everything was normal. Instead of returning to the holding area, however, he grabbed a couple of full 30 round magazines. He then went to a parked Hummvee which he took and drove back to the barracks area. He walked calmly to the back of the mess hall where he worked and shot his sleeping mess sergeant in the chest, killing him instantly. He continued to shoot randomly as he exited the mess hall, injuring several more soldiers. His First Sergeant, who happened to be nearby, heard the gunfire and began to chase him. The young soldier ran at first but then stopped abruptly and turned the weapon on himself.

A memorial ceremony was held for the murdered sergeant and was attended by hundreds of people. The command did not wish to honor the soldier who did the killing with a memorial ceremony due to the circumstances of his death which brought discredit to himself and the army. The general in command of the division approved the exception to policy. As a side note, the commander allowed for an unpublicized memorial service to be conducted in deference to the close friends of the dishonored soldier in order to help them get closure.

The change in the regulation was made in 2010 due to the widely varying practices within the Army at the time. Depending on who the installation or division commander was at the time, some soldiers who died by suicide were not allowed to have a memorial ceremony while others were. Some were allowed to have a ceremony, but without any honors being included. The change in regulation is an example of measures the Army is implementing to reduce the stigma associated with suicide in order to encourage soldiers contemplating suicide to seek help.

Memorial ceremonies are the responsibility of the commander. The unit staff is responsible for many of the aspects of the ceremony, but the chaplain is normally the subject matter expert.

The days following the loss of a soldier in the unit are critical for caring and understanding. It is perhaps the most difficult time for a chaplain, invariably under stress from inside and outside expectations and responsibilities. The chaplain and his assistant are usually very busy with all the details involved. Through all the business, however, the chaplain must bear in mind that he is the chaplain, and more often than not, the only chaplain to all who are involved.

Families are almost always invited to their loved one's memorial ceremony, sometimes at the expense of the unit. Families who attend are normally given reserved seating at the front and allowed to proceed forward to the memorial first. All that being true, remember that the memorial ceremony is a unit function for the members of the unit.

2 CEREMONY PLANNING

There are two extremes that people tend to gravitate toward when it comes to planning. The one is apt to befall the person that hates to plan. With enough head knowledge to wing it, he wants to get right to the doing and not waste time with tedious details. The danger in that approach is that he may find himself with no time or resources in the middle of the doing, saying, "Oops, I forgot the..."

The other extreme is for the person who loves to plan. He carefully scrutinizes every inch and every moment looking for the risk that something may go wrong. The danger in that approach is not actually getting anything done because the plan is not finished. It's best to be mindful of the necessity of both planning and doing.

The best time to plan for a memorial ceremony is long before a soldier dies. After a soldier dies it's too late to start planning with any hope of having a good ceremony since memorial ceremonies are typically conducted three to five days following the loss. There's more than enough to do to prepare for the actual event besides coming up with the plan.

Major commands in the Army have a Standard Operating Procedure (SOP) to conduct a memorial ceremony. These SOP's standardize ceremonies throughout the command that are most often conducted at the Battalion or Brigade level. The senior command SOP is general enough to allow for some flexibility with the intention of permitting the immediate commander to tailor the content and character of the ceremony to the needs of his unit.

A unit level memorial SOP allows the staff to learn and understand their part of the ceremony so they can be prepared when the time comes to execute. In contrast to the senior command SOP, the unit level document should be specific enough to handle almost all the details. It should also include checklists of what needs to be done by whom and templates of the bulletin.

When a soldier dies and a ceremony is needed, a planning meeting can resolve issues that the SOP, by necessity, is unable to address, such as the exact location, date and time, and putting names to positions. A good planning meeting will involve only those needed to attend. Too many people at the meeting increases the danger of chasing rabbits. A good planning meeting is long enough to set the ceremony in motion, but not so long as to drag on unproductively.

While the First Sergeant or Sergeant Major and chaplain are usually the subject matter experts on memorial ceremonies, other staff elements are subject matter experts in their own areas where they may contribute. The personnel section, for example, is responsible for maintaining personal information about the soldier and may be responsible for some of the content for the bulletin. They may also be responsible for having the bulletin published.

The operations section is normally responsible for military ceremonies in general and can guide the form and flow of the ceremony. A good operations section is capable of taking charge and running the entire ceremony, leaving the chaplain free to concentrate on the spiritual and pastoral aspects of the ceremony and the situation at hand. At a minimum, the operations staff should be consulted in developing the operations order (OPORD) or the fragment order (FRAGO) for the specific ceremony which is developed from the SOP.

The supply section can facilitate the location of the ceremony and may be responsible for the equipment used, such as the bayonet, boots, Kevlar, and stand. In some cases, the supply staff has direct control of a building suitable to use for the ceremony. If not, it is wise to be prepared to use a backup location if the primary facility is unavailable. As part of the planning process, coordinate with the owners of both a primary and backup facility for possible future use. Chapels generally give priority to memorial ceremonies, but plan for alternate locations as well. An unusually large ceremony may require an auditorium or theatre. In hostile fire zones, memorial ceremonies have been conducted in locations such as mess tents, aircraft hangers and maintenance bays when the chapel was too small or too remote. A smaller ceremony can be done equally effectively outdoors, weather and tactical situation permitting.

The location of the ceremony will affect the planning. A large ceremony that the family is able to attend may involve traffic control, parking, accommodations and transportation for the family, and similar issues. A high profile ceremony may involve coordination with the installation protocol office and civilian dignitaries who want to attend. A ceremony conducted on a forward base in a hostile fire zone may involve security and tactical constraints.

The culmination of the planning process is the rehearsal. The rehearsal may expose small issues the plan doesn't address like the mechanics involved when the speakers walk to the podium and back to their seat.

Prudence dictates that every memorial ceremony be rehearsed at least once no matter how proficient and experienced the participants. In the event the ceremony is the first in the unit for any of the key participants or if it has been some time since the last ceremony, then it should be rehearsed more than once. A dress rehearsal is a good way to make sure the ushers, firing party, and others will meet the expectations the commander has for their appearance. All the speakers should rehearse their remarks.

The greater the effort put into the planning, the better and easier the ceremony will be to conduct. It follows that a poor, hastily thrown together plan will likely result in a poor ceremony as well.

Planning can also be the difference in soldiers and family members leaving the ceremony feeling honored and having some measure of comfort and closure, or in leaving the ceremony feeling disappointed and hurt.

Take the time, put forth a diligent effort and come up with a first-rate plan.

3 CEREMONY SETUP

The setup for a memorial ceremony should be graphically documented in the SOP with a floor plan. When setting up the room for a memorial ceremony several things should be taken into account. The national colors are invariably present. When they are the only colors, they should be at the front, and from the speaker's perceptive, on the right (on the left side of the room from the audience's perspective). The flag is considered to be on the speaker platform and always has that position. When more than one flag is present, the national colors are on their own right. If possible, they should be on a nine foot flagstaff while other colors and guidons are displayed on an eight foot flagstaff. If the colors are displayed using a stand that crosses the flagstaffs, the national colors should wind up on their own right with their flagstaff in front of the other.

When arranging the seating, decide if the speakers will sit on the platform behind or to the side of the podium or in front of the platform with the audience. Normally, seating is reserved for the family, distinguished visitors, and the members of the fallen soldier's unit. Memorial ceremonies are high visibility events within the military. It is not at all uncommon for generals in the chain of command or even visiting generals and dignitaries to be in attendance. General officers have a protocol staff that can assist with the seating of distinguished visitors.

Entering and exiting the ceremony in an orderly manner must also be taken into account when arranging the seating. Normally at the conclusion of the ceremony, the attendees are given an opportunity to come forward to the memorial display and pay their last respects. Exiting the room from that point can be accomplished using a side door or an aisle separate from the aisle being used by those coming forward. It is helpful to have ushers direct the flow into and out of the ceremony.

The memorial display is the focal point of the ceremony setup. It consists of a stand, a bayoneted rifle with dog tags, a Kevlar, and a pair of combat boots.

The stand is basically a wooden box with a slit in the top surface to accommodate the bayonet fixed onto the rifle. It is normally large enough to place the boots on as well. Many chapels have generic stands that are available for units to borrow.

The unit may provide its own stand instead of using a generic one, thereby enhancing the honor paid to the unit and the atmosphere of the ceremony in general. Infantry units, for example, may want a light blue box with the unit crest painted on the front. An engineer unit could incorporate red for the sides with a gold engineer castle either painted or carved and attached on the front. The stand can also be made large enough to hold additional items such as a vase with a yellow rose or a framed picture of the soldier. Talented carpenter hobbyists within the unit are usually happy to help.

The bayonet of the rifle, most commonly an M-16, is inserted into the slit on the top of the stand so that the rifle is standing up on its muzzle with the pistol grip facing the audience. The deceased soldier's dog tags are hung from the pistol grip and the Kevlar rests on top, balanced on the stock of the weapon.

The combat boots are positioned on the stand with the heels in front of the weapon and the toes facing the audience. They may be placed together, or at a 45 degree angle indicating the position of attention. There is no official guidance one way or the other, though some soldiers have strong opinions on which way they should be. It's not worth making an issue over. Let the First Sergeant or Sergeant Major decide, and be happy with that. There are plenty of examples of each from ceremonies conducted by major commands.

The memorial display is normally centered at the front of the ceremony. It should be accessible by the audience when they come forward to pay their last respects for two reasons. First, it is customary for commanders and senior noncommissioned officers to place their coin on the stand. And second, it is a comfort to friends and family if they are able to touch the memorial in some way.

Other elements that could be considered for the set-up are arrangements of flowers or the display of something that represents the unit such as a unique sculpture or framed picture.

Wisdom suggests setting up the location as much in advance as possible. It is a real bonus if the dress rehearsal can be conducted in the location exactly as it will appear for the ceremony.

4 CEREMONY CONTENT

Commanders have wide discretion in determining what will be included in a memorial ceremony in their command. This freedom is almost always delegated down to the lowest levels of command. Only two elements of a ceremony are virtually guaranteed, some form of memorial tribute delivered and Taps. In hostile fire zones, it is not uncommon for the ceremony to eliminate the firing of volleys, which otherwise is also virtually guaranteed.

The optimal duration of a memorial ceremony is about 30 minutes. When deciding on the content, remember that every element takes time. Singing a hymn, for example, takes about 3 minutes, or one tenth of the allotted time. Speakers are usually allowed 3 to 5 minutes. Putting too many elements into a ceremony can make it too long. Remember what is important, and decide judiciously what to include and what to leave out.

The ceremony is a command responsibility; therefore, the commander has the final say as to what is included or excluded.

Honors

Colors

The presence of the American flag is an honor. Its absence in a memorial ceremony is an intentional slap in the face and communicates the command's disdain for the soldier. This honor can be embellished by having the colors posted at the beginning of the ceremony by a color guard. Posting the colors takes time, however. It is perfectly acceptable to have the colors in position before the start of the ceremony. The honor can also be enhanced by the color's proximity to the memorial display.

National Anthem

If the colors are posted by a color guard, it follows that the national anthem is played or sung.

Volleys

The firing of three volleys at the conclusion of the ceremony is a customary part of military ceremonies conducted in the Army. The Drill and Ceremonies Field Manual directs that the firing team consist of no more than eight soldiers and no fewer than five. While the three volleys are often fired by a firing party of seven soldiers, it is not a 21 gun salute. The 21 gun salute predates the founding of our country. It is a customary greeting for visiting heads of state and customarily done with cannon fire. Before the advent of air travel, it was often delivered with ships' cannons.

The three volleys fired in a memorial ceremony are derived from a practice in the civil war. When a civil war battle raged on for countless hours and sometimes days, time out was occasionally called in order to collect the dead and wounded from the battlefield. When each side was finished taking care of their dead and wounded, they would fire three shots into the air to signal the other side that they had taken care of their casualties and were ready to resume the battle.

Taps

Taps is another part of the ceremony that dates back to the Civil War. While there are several different versions of how Taps came to be, the account supported by West Point Military Academy attributes the melody to Union Army Brigadier General Daniel Butterfield while at Harrison's Landing in Virginia in July 1862. According to the general and his bugler, Butterfield wrote the tune and worked with his bugler, Oliver W. Norton, to perfect it. Butterfield was not happy with the contemporary lights out bugle call and wrote Taps to use in its place. Captain John C. Tidball, also at Harrison's landing at the time, is credited with the first use of the tune for a military funeral. He was told that the tactical situation at the time prevented using the firing of the volleys, so he substituted Taps in their place.

Taps is played after the firing of the volleys and marks the conclusion of the ceremony.

Roll Call

The roll call, or final roll call, is a powerful addition to a memorial ceremony. It is one of the unit traditions that has become a popular part of ceremonies today.

The roll call uses three soldiers, preselected from the deceased soldier's unit, and the unit First Sergeant. After the conclusion of the speakers' remarks and a moment of silence, if used, the First Sergeant calls the deceased soldier's company to attention. He then calls out the names of the three soldiers who each answer his roll call. For example: "Specialist Snuffy!"

"Here, First Sergeant!"

After calling the three accomplices, The First Sergeant calls the name of the deceased using only the last name, "Private Doe". After a moment of silence, he calls his name again using the first and last name; "Private John Doe". After another moment of silence, he calls the name a third time using the full name; "Private John A. Doe". The First Sergeant waits a moment then returns to his seat.

An alternate method would be for the company commander to go to the front of the formation and stand behind the First Sergeant. Then, after the name of the fallen soldier is called the third time, the First Sergeant turns and faces the commander, salutes, and reports, loud enough that the audience can hear, that Private Doe did not answer roll call.

Final Salute

The final salute is an honor also commonly used in ceremonies. The likelihood of the soldier having a local funeral is remote in an active duty unit and impossible in a combat zone; therefore, most of the unit will not have an opportunity to attend. The final salute is performed at the conclusion of the ceremony, after Taps. Members of the audience are invited to come forward to the memorial and pay their last respects. The final salute may be their only opportunity to say goodbye.

The family, if present, is normally invited first, followed by distinguished visitors, and then the members of the unit followed by anyone else who wishes to come forward. For small ceremonies with no family present, time may allow one person to come down at a time. In a larger ceremony, ushers can guide groups of two or four persons at a time.

Prior to the memorial ceremony, members of the unit should be instructed to render a proper memorial salute. From the position of attention, the soldier slowly brings his right hand up to the salute position, taking about three seconds. He holds the salute for a second, then taking another three seconds, lowers his hand back to the position of attention.

Common Elements

In addition to the ceremonial honors rendered, there are potentially unscripted parts of the ceremony that are commonly used. To keep the ceremony close to 30 minutes, time constraints may be required, as speaking parts by themselves can fill up the entire time.

Invocation

Even though a memorial ceremony is an official military ceremony, an invocation by the chaplain is often included. From the Latin words meaning "to call in," an invocation is a prayer that calls upon the presence of God and asks His blessing. It can be accomplished in few words, saving precious time for the important tribute to come.

As with all prayers conducted for any military ceremony, the prayer should be inclusive in nature. From the first word spoken to the final salute, remember that the goal of the ceremony is to bring honor and closure in response to the death of a soldier. The last thing a chaplain should want is to offend a grieving member of the unit that, otherwise, may have sought his counsel.

Eulogy

A brief biography, service record, or a combination of

the two is usually included as part of the ceremony. It is usually read by the commander as part of his remarks if it is read aloud. To save time, it can be printed in the bulletin. As part of the bulletin, everyone will have it to read and take with them, and it most certainly will be read.

Most units that deploy collect biographical information on their soldiers and take their picture before they leave. The personnel section keeps this information in the event it must be used for a memorial ceremony. Most of the soldiers comply, fill out the information cards and return them to the unit. Invariably, the soldier that died, Private Murphy, is the one that either was sick that day and didn't fill out the card or whose card got lost for one reason or another. When units in that situation are deployed, they do their best to gather what information they can from friends and the soldier's record.

There is a relatively easy way to gather accurate and pertinent information to ensure the eulogy is complete. When a soldier dies, the defense department has 24 hours in which to notify the designated relatives. After notification, an official Department of Defense press release announces the death. Once the defense department public affairs office has issued the release, hometown press agencies are free to release the news. Within a day or two, extensive biographical information can be found on the internet, courtesy of the soldier's local news reporters and media.

By checking those sources, an accurate eulogy can be prepared which decreases the chances that a close relative will be omitted or the birthplace or high school name will be wrong. It has happened before.

Speakers

The meat of the memorial ceremony is the message

delivered by the speakers. Appropriate persons to speak at a memorial ceremony are the commander or his representative, a close friend of the deceased, and the chaplain. If a ceremony is conducted for more than one soldier, an additional friend for each of the deceased soldiers can speak.

Command. The commander speaks from the perspective of losing one of his soldiers. He brings out the duty aspect of the soldier's life; his contribution and importance to the unit and the mission. It's important that the commander also share some personal anecdote of his experience with the soldier. That lets the family and friends know that their loved one was important and known by the command. It also adds authenticity to the presence of distinguished visitors.

Friend. A good friend of the deceased brings out the human side of the soldier. Often, it will be the friend that brings a little levity to an otherwise somber and heavy atmosphere. They will probably be unaccustomed to public speaking and need coaching. It follows then that their remarks should be written out and looked over and approved before the ceremony. Have them rehearse the remarks with someone else or in front of a mirror. One method of coaching is to take the written remarks and read them back to the friend, illustrating voice inflection and the use of appropriate pauses to make it more interesting and authentic for the audience.

Chaplain. The chaplain brings the memorial tribute message. As he prepares the tribute he should be cognizant of several things. The message in a memorial ceremony should be ecumenical instead of denominational as it is meant for all who are present. The message should bring some form of closure to the shock of losing a friend and loved one. In that context, the audience expects the chaplain to be the chaplain. He is expected to bring a word from God without being preachy or reproving.

Public speakers, including clergy, have different means to assist them during the delivery of the message. At one extreme is the speaker that uses nothing, shoots from the hip and says whatever comes to mind at the moment of delivery. Then some use an outline or brief notes to keep them on track and help them remember everything they prepared. At the other extreme are speakers that read from a text.

Since time is always a critical element in a memorial ceremony, the safest way to deliver the memorial message is from a manuscript. This keeps the speaker focused and should eliminate going on and on, getting sidetracked on something unrelated to the message.

Before the ceremony, read the text deliberately a minimum of three times. It may help to use a large font and double space, so as much eye contact can be kept with the audience as possible while still being able to follow the manuscript.

The memorial tribute should be focused and communicate something of value. If the message is important enough to deliver at such a critical and visible time, it should be important enough to remember. Most chaplains studied message delivery during the course of their training and learned a widely taught axiom: condense the essence of the message down to a single sentence. This simple trick also helps keep the message interesting and easy to remember. Wandering from subject to subject confuses the listener who may well stop listening out of exasperation.

There are many themes that can be used as the substance of the message. A few possible themes are:

- Life is short, make it count.
- God loves us and will see us through the pain of loss.

- Sergeant Doe was a hero in the truest sense of the word and deserves our admiration.
- No greater love has any man than to give his life in service for his friends.
- We are in an epic battle against an evil enemy that we will ultimately prevail against.
- Our strength comes from God who gives us the strength to die and the strength to live.
- We will never forget our comrade who paid the ultimate price for our freedom.
- There is a time for everything, joy, mourning, hope, etc.

There are many other themes that are also appropriate; the point is, don't try and use them all in one memorial message. Pick a theme, develop it, illustrate it, and explain it so a child could understand the message. Develop the message with the goal of holding the audience's attention instead of boring them out of their minds.

Today's chaplain is likely to conduct more than one memorial ceremony for the same audience. For that reason alone the chaplain should have more than one message prepared. If the chaplain is good, he will read the mood of the unit and develop a message that hits at the heart of what they need to hear. Every unit is a little different in that respect, and their mood may also be a result of the circumstances of the soldier's death.

A video was made some years back at a large installation as a training video for memorial ceremonies. The chaplain speaking, however, chased rabbits, talked of numerous unrelated personal anecdotes and went on for well over half an hour. The audience, seated in a large chapel, seemed to be listening attentively, but when the video was played in fast forward the audience appeared to come alive like a squirming caterpillar. Shifting their seating position back and forth and from side to side, they were clearly uncomfortable and probably bored.

The ultimate goal of the memorial message is to convey some sort of truth to the audience they need and will remember. It is preferable for them to sit, listen attentively, and leave thinking, "wow", rather than to have them sit and only be thinking about getting out of there and never coming back to hear "that guy" again. An audience interested in what is being said will also be more forgiving if the message lasts a few more minutes.

It's a good idea to start the message off with a good attention grabber. Reading dramatically the passage in Isaiah 40, for example, that begins with *"Have ye not known? Have ye not heard?"* It's OK to use relevant and inclusive scripture in the message. Isaiah 40 talks about the power and majesty of God. Save John 14 for another setting; it is exclusively Christian and not appropriate for a military ceremony of any kind. While there are many universal truths communicated in scripture, it is not required to use, and it is possible to effectively communicate the message in other ways. The first sample message at the end of this book doesn't quote any scripture.

As with any good message, tie it up at the end with a conclusion that sums up the idea you are trying to convey. A chaplain once did a memorial ceremony where the theme was the tragedy of losing a soldier due to an accident. He began the message by drawing attention to a sign near the front gate that had a red light which flashed for two days whenever a soldier died in a vehicle accident. After talking about the value of life, the tragedy of the accident, and our tendency to take it all for granted, the final line of the message was: "A light at the front gate flashes whenever a soldier dies in an accident; today the light flashes for Specialist John Doe."

Make the message as relevant as possible by including references to current events. The president and other leaders are frequently in the news and quoted saying something of use. Hollywood produces a steady stream of patriotic and military themed material.

I watched the 20th Century Fox movie, *Live Free or Die Hard,* just after it was released and was thrilled at how perfectly a short discussion between the two main characters epitomized what I wanted to say in an upcoming memorial ceremony. With no other way to get a copy of the lines I wanted to quote, I wrote the studio directly. They responded, sending me the lines I needed and added at the end, "Thank you for your request, and we wish you well at the memorial ceremony."

There are many sites on the Internet where quotes can be found. To find a relevant quote, it's simple to use a search engine to search for the quote directly or alternatively to search for a quote site. Some sites arrange quotes by subject, which makes it easier to find something appropriate. Many sites that review movies in general also include a section where various quotes from a movie can be found.

Using quotes from other sources helps make the message interesting to the audience. But remember to take the time, do the research and do the honorable thing, which is to give credit to the person you're quoting. It's more respectable than saying that someone once said, and there's a good chance that someone sitting and listening to you will already know who said what you are quoting.

The optimum time for the chaplain's message is around ten minutes. Much less than ten minutes and there is the risk of not saying anything meaningful. Much more than ten minutes and time may become the issue instead of the message. The cold, hard truth to remember is that nobody came to hear the chaplain speak. They came to say goodbye to their friend, comrade, and loved one. The most effective chaplain will help them do that.

After the conclusion of the chaplain's remarks is an

appropriate time for a silent tribute. It helps the flow if the chaplain simply asks the audience to pause in silence in memory of the fallen. This can be done seated or standing. If the audience is seated, the final roll call which usually follows is more dramatic since the members of the unit will be called to attention.

Additional Elements

Music

Music is not required for a memorial ceremony beyond the playing of Taps. Music, if used, can enhance the setting and mood of the ceremony. Even in hostile fire zones one can usually locate electronic keyboards, musicians and instruments of all kinds. A prelude of soft keyboard music can be used to set the tone as people are entering the facility before the ceremony. A postlude can also be used in the background as people are moving toward the memorial to pay their last respects.

Hymn. A hymn is optional for a memorial ceremony and only takes two to three minutes to sing. If a hymn is used, it should be patriotic and inclusive such as "America, the Beautiful", or "My Country 'tis of Thee."

Special Music. Special music can also be a potent element in a memorial ceremony. Music used by funeral homes is usually appropriate for memorial ceremonies as well. Special music can be provided by an accompanied soloist, group, or done instrumentally. Opening the ceremony with "Amazing Grace" played by a bagpiper, for example, creates a moving and memorable experience.

Prayer

A memorial prayer can be included in the ceremony. It can be prayed by the chaplain just before or just after his remarks. It can also be prayed by a volunteer at an earlier place in the ceremony. In either case it needs to follow the same rules as the invocation and for the same reasons. It is possible to do a benediction, but awkward. After the firing of the volleys, Taps is played. A benediction at that time would precede the final salute implying that it is not important. After the final salute, no one is left in the facility to receive the benediction.

Service Award

Some units present a posthumous award to the deceased during the ceremony. If time permits, this act enhances the honor paid to the soldier. To save time, a posthumous award can also be displayed as part of the memorial in a separate picture frame. The award citation can also be printed in the bulletin, creating a lasting memory of the honor.

Scripture

A scripture passage is also appropriate for use in a ceremony, as long as it follows the guidelines for prayer in that it is inclusive. The 23rd Psalm, for example, can be read either by the chaplain or by a volunteer from the unit. To save time, it can also be printed in the bulletin. Printing the scripture so that it takes up the back page of the bulletin sets it distinctively apart.

Bulletin

The bulletin, if used, is one of the most important elements of the ceremony. Even from a combat zone, a copy of the bulletin is normally sent to the family of the fallen soldier. If the bulletin is thrown together without any effort having gone into its creation, the embarrassment to the unit or hurt to the family will remain. The family, friends, and distant relatives of the memorialized soldier will look at the bulletin for years to come. A sloppy bulletin can undermine an otherwise wonderful ceremony.

There are no formal rules for the bulletin. A regular church bulletin format is used for the order of events. The bulletin can have as many pages as are required to convey the information. In addition to the order of events, the bulletin can include such things as pictures, biography, scripture, awards, and a memoriam of fellow soldiers fallen in the current deployment. Bulletins come in multiples of four pages: right and left sides of front and back. If five or six pages are needed for the eulogies, order of events and cover, the rest can be used for such things as a short unit history, where some of the elements in the ceremony originated, or simply display a relevant picture. A blank page is boring. Put something interesting and relevant on it.

It is no small task to ensure the accuracy of the bulletin. Our own brain works against it. Many years ago, a paragraph circulated around the internet and through e-mails. The paragraph had a significant number of letters jumbled up in the words throughout. Despite the mixed up letters, it was fairly easy to read due to a special kind of optical illusion where the brain fills in what's missing. The same optical illusion works in the minds of those that proofread memorial ceremony bulletins.

When units had been notified they were deploying to Saudi Arabia in the first Gulf War, a certain chaplain, responsible for his battalion newsletter, decided to print a special edition announcing the event. In large bold print, the headline read simply: "Dessert Storm!" After the newsletter was ready for printing, the chaplain, his wife, the battalion commander, and his wife, all educated people, each individually proofread it. Then 300 copies were printed, the first copy going to the commander. He took it and immediately asked, "Are we going to Desert Storm, or Dessert Storm." The moral of the story: no amount of proofreading is too much.

Spelling mistakes with the word processors we have today are a thing of the past. Some programs automatically correct spelling without any notice. One of the goals of proofreading is to catch the "worlds" that are spelled correctly but are not the "words" that we intended. Remember, it's a deliberate process because our brains are working against us.

Besides the technical mistakes involving grammar and spelling, the most common content errors made in a bulletin include dates being wrong, places being wrong, surviving family members left out, and numbers not adding up; i.e. a nineteen year old soldier with ten years of military service. A common source of content errors is the information in the sample template used to create the bulletin. Take the time and get it right. Imagine being a family member and receiving the bulletin.

5 SAMPLE MEMORIAL CEREMONY MESSAGES

The following are messages from actual military memorial ceremonies. The names of the fallen soldiers have been changed.

I. Soldier's Life had Significance

Edward Everett, former United States Congressman, Senator, President of Harvard University, United States Ambassador to Britain, Governor of Massachusetts and United States Secretary of State under President Millard Fillmore was asked to dedicate the Soldier's National Cemetery at Gettysburg, Pennsylvania.

On November 19th, 1863, looking over the battlefield where 46 thousand American soldiers were killed and 27 thousand wounded, he spoke these words which are as true today as the day they were delivered, one hundred and fifty years ago. *"I feel, as never before, how justly, from the dawn of history to the present time, men have paid the homage of their gratitude and admiration to the memory of those who nobly sacrifice their lives that their fellow-men may live in safety and in honor. And if this tribute were ever due, to whom could it*

be more justly paid than to those whose last resting-place
we this day commend to the blessing of Heaven and of
men?"

This story began several years ago when on Sept. 11, 2001, we watched in awe and shock at the almost surreal pictures of a large airliner plowing into one of the towers of the World Trade Center. We watched on in shock and disbelief as another and then another airliner crashed into the second World Trade Center Tower and the Pentagon. Rumors began to fly as the magnitude of the evil we faced as a nation began to sink in. We were horrified by the loss of lives. Our hearts quickly became troubled. We realized, in concrete terms, that ruthless men filled with hate didn't play by the rules. We learned painfully that we as a nation can never let down our guard against corruption and tyranny, no matter how distant from our shores.

Today we understand well that terrorists attacked our homeland and fully intend to destroy our way of life. If they had their way, they would demolish our technology and bring the world back into a dark age to be ruled by greedy, self-serving despots. If they had their way, they would eradicate free expression and eliminate all we know of art, music, literature, and theater to force us to live life as mindless servants. Thankfully, Americans will not stand for that.

After the cowardly attack on our homeland, young men volunteered in record numbers all across America; strong young men whose hearts swelled with patriotism; brave young men driven with a fervor of vindication. As if with a single voice, they unanimously put the enemy on notice. Our guard is up, and we're bringing the fight to your doorstep.

Every man strives to make his life count for something. Some, by building or creating something that bears their name and will remain after they are gone. Some pursue fame or notoriety so they will be remembered. Many, soldiers in particular, signify their lives by being a part of something bigger than themselves, something honorable, and something worthy.

The men of this brigade were promised before they left that their experience in combat would make them better men. They are now indeed a part of a great work, the essence of which will make the whole world a better place. As they fulfill their duty, they see firsthand the ravages of tyranny and the consequences of hate. Their hearts go out to the innocent victims, the casualties of war. They are finding a new appreciation for the peace and freedom we experience here at home, peace and freedom we enjoy as part of the legacy left to us by soldiers who have gone before, peace and freedom our soldiers are in the midst of bequeathing to the people of Iraq. This story is not finished.

It seems like only yesterday we said goodbye in Memorial Gymnasium. Such a short time ago John Doe boarded that jet with a determined expression, knowing the dangers ahead, knowing the possibility that he might give his all, yet determined to do his duty. He placed service to our nation above his own personal safety. His sacrifice to establish and protect freedom embodies the noblest attributes of humankind. He and his comrades serve as a gallant example to the rest of the world that honor and integrity are attainable. His sacrifice is the proof of all that America stands for.

We honor SGT Doe this morning because he is a member of a special class of people. He is among the best citizens our nation has to offer. And just as we go forward with the legacy we inherited from a long line of American soldiers; the legacy of SGT Doe lives on through the lives of those he left behind.

President Lincoln also spoke at the dedication of the Soldiers National Cemetery that brisk November day. He said, *"Memorials are for the living, reminders that men and women died so that others might be free."* And so we are gathered here to remember that John Doe died so that others might be free.

John's life is now in the hands of God. He is beyond the reach of pain and disappointment. And it's only a matter of time before we all will be reunited beyond death's door. For now John will live on in everyone who knew him.

Those of us who are old enough will never forget where we were or what we were doing when President Kennedy was assassinated, neither will we forget that moment when the shuttle Challenger exploded. We will never forget where we were or what we were doing when four planes hijacked by terrorists ended in such tragedy, and we will not forget the sacrifice of our comrade, a brother, a son, a husband and father, John Doe.

Now let our actions prove he did not die in vain.

II. Soldier Gave His All in Selfless Service for a Righteous Cause

Hast thou not known? Hast thou not heard, that the everlasting God, the LORD, the Creator of the ends of the earth, fainteth not, neither is weary? There is no searching of his understanding. He giveth power to the faint; and to them that have no might he increaseth strength. Even the youths shall faint and be weary, and the young men shall utterly fall: But they that wait upon the Lord shall renew their strength; they shall mount up with wings as eagles; they shall run, and not be weary; and they shall walk, and not faint.

This morning we gather here to honor and celebrate the lives of three young men who gave their lives so others, strangers to them, might enjoy a better life and a life free from cruelty. They fought and made the supreme sacrifice in the war on tyranny and oppression in which we are presently engaged. The story began several years ago when on Sept. 11, 2001, we watched in awe and shock at the almost surreal scene of large airliners crashing into the towers of World Trade Center and the Pentagon. Rumors began to fly as the magnitude of the evil we faced as a nation began to sink in. We were stunned by the devastation. Our nation realized in a tangible way that ruthless men controlled by hate didn't play by the rules. The painfully learned lesson impelled strong young men whose hearts swelled with patriotism. Brave young men driven with the fervor of vindication volunteered to take the fight to a desolate distant land. As if with a single voice they unanimously put the enemy on notice. We will not tolerate your hatred and injustice here or there.

The enemy will not win this fight. American soldiers

do not cower or shrink in dismay. It is against their very nature. Instead, each injustice and cowardly act by the enemy strengthens the determination to win. After the attack on Pearl Harbor, though not a direct quote, admiral Isoroku Yamamoto is credited with saying, *"I fear all we have done is to awaken a sleeping giant and fill him with a terrible resolve,"* a thought that the Taliban and Al Qaeda must be pondering to some extent today. Soldiers are making it happen.

From biblical times until now the soldier has always been highly respected, since the values that people in general strive for are lived out every day in the life of a soldier. The over-riding theme in all soldier values is the concept of selfless service; putting other's needs first. There is no higher calling. And part of the reason our hearts ache today is that these soldiers have achieved what God has called all men to; selfless service. It makes their loss so much more difficult to bear.

Today we venerate authentic American heroes, and Americans are grateful for their lives. Sure, there are some people who don't understand, who refuse to see beyond their own interests. But what credit is there in ingratitude. Across the Internet, these young men's names and their stories can be found on thousands of web pages paying them homage, sites created by thousands of people from every walk of life and status wishing to convey their appreciation to men, so brave, as to say, *"If not me, who; if not now, when?"* The heart of America realizes that these men epitomize the highest ideals of our country.

We are the benefactors of a great legacy from the minutemen who fought to protect their farms and families, from the patriots at valley forge who took courage, pulled together and determined to survive, from the doughboys and yanks in European trenches and forests coming to the aid of friends and fighting to end oppression there, and American soldiers fighting for the freedom of the exploited masses in Asian jungles, rivers, deserts, and mountains. That legacy endured in the lives of these three men and lives on in the lives of those they left behind.

In the recent Dreamworks / Warner Brothers movie "Flags of Our Fathers," James Bradley, the son of one of the Marines who raised the famous flag at Iwo Jima, reflects on the battle and how it affected the young men who fought there. In closing he said, *"Heroes are something we create; something we need. It's a way for us to understand what is almost incomprehensible, how people could sacrifice so much for us. But for these men, the risks they took, the wounds they suffered, they did that for their buddies. They may have fought for their country, but they died for their friends, the man in front or the man beside them. And if we wish to truly honor these men, we should remember them the way they really were."* And I ask, who best can remember but we who are gathered in this auditorium this morning?

Though the time to say goodbye to these, our comrades, has been forced upon us, their memory will be with us forever. We feel the sorrow of losing them, but they are beyond the reach of pain and disappointment. Their lives are now in the hands of a merciful and loving God. And soon we all will be reunited beyond death's door. In the meantime, let us continue to honor them through our lives.

John Doe, Jim Doe, and Matt Doe: brothers, sons, husbands, fathers, and friends.

□

III. A Time for Everything

To every thing there is a season, and a time to every purpose under the heaven: a time to be born, and a time to die; a time to plant, and a time to pluck up that which is planted; a time to kill, and a time to heal; a time to break down, and a time to build up; a time to weep, and a time to laugh; a time to mourn, and a time to dance; a time to cast away stones, and a time to gather stones together; a time to embrace, and a time to refrain from embracing; a time to get, and a time to lose; a time to keep, and a time to cast away; a time to rend, and a time to sew; a time to keep silence, and a time to speak; a time to love, and a time to hate; a time of war, and a time of peace.

Today we find ourselves at a crossroads: half way between our memories and our dreams. We have gathered here this morning and set apart this time to honor Sergeant John Doe, taken in the prime of his life, the victim of a ruthless and spineless enemy.

This is a somber time. Sergeant Doe is a hero, and realizing that makes it all the more difficult to mourn the loss of our friend and comrade. He joined the Army in a time of war, knowing and understanding that he would go abroad to face the enemy. He went with friends, each willing to pay the ultimate price for our freedom. Is there any more gallant an act of bravery? Is there a more genuine example of self-sacrifice? Such great valor, so great a cost.

As we remember John this morning, we grieve for the loss of a brother in arms. A mother and father endure the loss of their son. Commanders at every level from Captain to General bear with aching hearts the death of this young man. They are reminded again of the grievous burden of their responsibilities.

This is a time of pride. Sergeant Doe is a hero. He embodied the compassion of America that reaches out to those too weak to defend themselves. He stood up to the tyranny of the oppressor when others would not or could not stand. He exemplified the highest and noblest principles of America that choose the right course of action, though it may be the more difficult. And, of course, he approached life as a true American with a strong sense of freedom and a passion for adventure.

On the 4th anniversary of the beginning of the war in Iraq, to mark the occasion, President Bush addressed the nation to give an update on the environment in Iraq and the progress of the mission there. He concluded with these words.

"I'm grateful to our service men and women for all they've done, for the honor they brought to their uniform and their country. I'm grateful to our military families for all the sacrifices they have made for our country. We also hold in our hearts the good men and women who've given their lives in this struggle. We pray for the loved ones they have left behind. The United States military is the most capable and courageous fighting force in the world. And whatever our differences in Washington, our troops and their families deserve the appreciation and the support of our entire nation."

This is a time to refocus. Today we find ourselves at a crossroads: half way between our memories and our dreams. Many travel this road of life and take it for granted, but at times like these we are reminded just how fragile life is. In due course we will all die. Life is short. We look forward to the day we will reunite with those who, like John, have gone before. In the meantime, perhaps we should concentrate our energy to invest in, and take full advantage of those things that endure: the relationships of friends and family; the concern and kindness we show to those around us; the reputation we leave behind. In other words, to follow the example that John followed in his life.

This is a time to say goodbye. With admiration and sorrow we bid farewell to SGT Doe. He is beyond the reach of pain and frustration in the hands of a loving and merciful God. The annals of history will remember him for his deeds, and his name will be inscribed in stone so America will never forget the debt we owe him. But we will remember him for the person he was and the life he shared. He will always live on in our memories - and our dreams.

The same God who received John draws near to us. His power to bring consolation and peace is unfathomable. And it is at these very times that He carries us.

The Lord bless thee, and keep thee:

The Lord make his face shine upon thee, and be gracious unto thee:

The Lord lift up his countenance upon thee, and give thee peace.

☐

IV. Cavalry Soldier's Heroic Courage in the Long Struggle Against Evil

In thee, O Lord, do I put my trust; let me never be ashamed: deliver me in thy righteousness. Bow down thine ear to me; deliver me speedily: be thou my strong rock, for an house of defence to save me. For thou art my rock and my fortress; therefore for thy name's sake lead me, and guide me. Pull me out of the net that they have laid privily for me: for thou art my strength. Into thine hand I commit my spirit: thou hast redeemed me, O Lord God of truth.

When President Lincoln spoke at the dedication of the cemetery at Gettysburg, Pennsylvania, he said we were *"engaged in a great civil war, testing whether"* our *"nation, or any nation so conceived and dedicated"* as we were, could *"long endure."* Today we are engaged in another kind of war, testing on a global scale the culmination of the ideals and values our nation stands for.

This war is, in a way, the culmination of a struggle that the Cavalry has been engaged in since its inception. The rapid expansion of our nation westward gave rise to outlaws and bandits that lived outside and beyond the reach of the law. There was a time when civilization stopped at the east bank of the Mississippi river. Cruel men, fueled only by their own desires and ambitions victimized the weak and the defenseless. Pioneers, explorers, adventurers and those looking for a better life in the west depended on the Cavalry to defend them. Those living on the edge of civilization depended on the Cavalry to protect them from raiders and marauders who struck from remote hiding places. In due time, however, every outlaw was hunted down.

Every hiding place was uncovered.

Today, the world is much smaller thanks to technology. Yet, that same technology makes it possible for cruel men, fueled only by their own desires and ambitions to strike at us from hiding places around the world. But the Cavalry is still on duty, tracking down outlaws, exposing hiding places, and teaching honest men in remote corners of the world how to do the same. It's only a matter of time.

True today more than ever is the resolution John Kennedy delivered at his inauguration in January 1961. *"Let every nation know, whether it wishes us well or ill, that we will pay any price, bear any burden, meet any hardship, support any friend, oppose any foe, in order to assure the survival and the success of Liberty."* To that purpose, the Cavalry is still on duty. For just as the old west had to be tamed to assure the safety and stability of our nation then, the wild and untamed recesses of the world must be brought within the reach of law and order to assure the safety and stability of our nation today. The task is of such magnitude that it can't be accomplished with a single command, but must be achieved by the day to day actions of heroes such as these three soldiers we honor this morning.

We get the word "hero" from the Greek word ἥρως (hey'roess). In Greek literature, a hero usually fulfills the definitions of what is considered good and noble in the originating culture. Typically the willingness to sacrifice himself for the greater good is seen as the most important defining characteristic of a hero.

The dictionary defines a hero as someone who commits an act of remarkable bravery or who has shown great courage, strength of character, or another admirable quality. Taking a closer look, we see that courage is at the heart of the definition: the ability to overcome fear in order to do the right thing; the ability to face danger, uncertainty, and pain.

Fear is such a driving force that it controls most people. Fear is the strongest human emotion and will take precedence over other emotions in a heartbeat. The one who overcomes fear is deserving of admiration. Nearly fifty years ago in a private journal entry, Ralph Waldo Emerson put it like this. *"Courage charms us, because it indicates that a man loves an idea better than all things in the world, that he is thinking neither of his bed, nor his dinner, nor his money, but will venture all to put in act the invisible thought of his mind."*

A hero demonstrates courage, and courage is not demonstrated easily. C.S. Lewis wrote in his book, "The Screwtape Letters", that, *"Courage is not simply one of the virtues, but the form of every virtue at the testing point."* In other words, a courageous person will be successful in every area of his life. Courage is the opposite of insecurity. It is the strength behind diligence and patience. It is the stability that allows the singleness of mind to pursue the right course of action. It is the simple essence of what a hero is.

Helen Keller, who at the age of 19 months was struck by an illness which left her deaf and blind, grew up to be a symbol of courage. She once said, *"I long to accomplish great and noble tasks, but it is my chief duty to accomplish humble tasks as though they were great and noble. The world is moved along, not only by the mighty shoves of its heroes, but also by the aggregate of the tiny pushes of each honest worker."* Helen Keller's picture appears on the Alabama quarter above the word courage, and she is honored today as a hero. She, like most heroes, did not consider herself to be one, though she graduated magna cum laud from Radcliff College; learned to read French, German, Greek, and Latin; became a world famous speaker and author of 12 books; and was awarded the Presidential Medal of Freedom by President Johnson.

If you ask an American soldier today if he is a hero, he will most likely say no. Nevertheless, he will have that hero attitude to accomplish humble tasks as if they were great and noble. He will face his fears and still hold true to his duty.

In a WWI cemetery in what was once Burma, on a stone honoring the soldiers who fought there is the simple epitaph, *"When You Go Home, Tell Them of Us and Say, For Your Tomorrow, We Gave Our Today."*

This morning we remember and honor Sergeant John Doe, Sergeant Jim Doe, and Private First Class Matt Doe, three Cavalry soldiers who gave their all for the struggle facing the world presently. They dedicated themselves to a greater good and are heroes in every sense of the word. For our tomorrow, they gave their today.

With heavy hearts we say goodbye, knowing that we can never repay. But the courage they lived by and the courage they died with will inspire us from now on.

☐

V. Soldier was a Hero and Deserves Our Admiration

Greater love hath no man than this, that a man lay down his life for his friends.

Fellow soldiers, friends, family, and guests of honor, we are here this morning to remember and honor the lives and sacrifice of Sergeant John Doe and Private First Class Jim Doe. These two young men didn't wear capes, probably wouldn't stand out in a crowd at the mall. They were young, full of energy, and they loved life. They loved making other people smile. They loved their families; they loved their friends; and they loved their country.

We honor these two soldiers now because they are special. And for the price they paid on our behalf, it is fitting that we pay back to them this honor and this respect. It is not our way to leave behind a fallen comrade, nor is it our way to forget our heroes.

Hero! That portrayal is used so freely and lightly today. Just what is a hero? F. Scott Fitzgerald said, *"The goal of the hero is to return life to the living."*

A hero may be motivated by an honorable cause that is overlooked or unpopular. Or he may be motivated by some great injustice perpetrated by an arch villain or force. For example, the pain and indignation that we all felt when innocent civilians were murdered en mass in New York City nearly six years ago.

But motivation alone does not make a hero. A hero is part motivation, part devotion, and part ability. To move from being motivated to being a hero requires courage. How often do we fail to realize a potential due to fear or insecurity. A hero pushes forward with such a strong desire to do what is right, that fear and doubt are driven away. Courage is one of the things that set these two apart and merits our admiration.

To move from being motivated to being a hero also requires ability, not just the strength and means to accomplish, but an attitude that doesn't make excuses. William Booth, the founder of the Salvation Army put it this way. *"Without excuse and self-consideration of health or limb or life; true soldiers fight, live to fight, love the thickest of the fight, and die in the midst of it."*

The most essential ingredient of a hero is self-sacrifice. We all have an idea of what that means: skipping dessert in order to lose a few pounds; tightening the budget to save up for something expensive. People routinely set priorities in their lives and make sacrifices to reach their goals. A hero is set apart by the sacrifices they make for others for no more gain than the knowledge and satisfaction of their accomplishment.

Former Chairman of the Joint Chiefs of Staff, Colin Powell, describes General of the Army George Marshall as such a man. *"The quiet power of the man lay in his utter selflessness ... in the dignity ... in his hard work and his immense personal sacrifice ... in his compassion, his wisdom. ... Yet he would have thought it odd if you had tried to congratulate him for these things. To him, those virtues were simply expected of a citizen of this country."*

A hero is not simply someone who performs a heroic act. Heroes live their lives thinking of others. They are aware inwardly of the right and the noble. The acts of heroism are the proof of the character of the hero.

In the 2004 Columbia Pictures movie, Spider-man 2, Mary Parker tries to encourage her nephew Peter with these words. *"Lord knows, kids like Henry need a hero: Courageous, self-sacrificing people, setting examples for all of us. Everybody loves a hero: people line up for them; cheer them; scream their names. And years later, they'll tell how they stood in the rain for hours just to get a glimpse of the one who taught them how to hold on a second longer. I believe there's a hero in all of us, that keeps us honest, gives us strength, makes us noble, and finally allows us to die with pride, even though sometimes we have to be steady, and give up the thing we want the most; even our dreams. "*

Sergeant Doe and Private First Class Doe have shown us by their many actions that they are truly heroes. For love of country they answered the call. They went to Iraq in the place of those who would not go. They went to fight in the place of those who could not go. Their hearts and thoughts were not only toward their comrades, but of their family and friends back home. And for them they made many a sacrifice.

We honor these young men this morning for being the heroes they were. It is fitting that we pay back to them this honor and this respect.

VI. Grief and Fear are Overcome by Love

(Begin the ceremony with the words to "The Ragged Old Flag" by Johnny Cash)
"I walked through a county courthouse square; on a park bench an old man was sitting there...

... On second thought I DO like to brag, 'cause I'm mighty proud of that Ragged Old Flag."

Only two weeks ago we celebrated the 231st birthday of our nation. And in that celebration we remembered the tyranny our forefathers defeated. We commemorated the victories and accomplishments of American heroes throughout our history. The heroes we honor today will take their place in the annals of history being written at this very moment.

This morning I would like to examine the other side of heroic sacrifice. The personal side, the less talked about side; we who remain and have suffered the loss of our friends, our family.

Early in The Fellowship of the Ring by JRR Tolkien, the character Frodo realizes that his task is gravely difficult. In the darkness of a cave he tells Gandalf, *"I wish the ring had never come to me. I wish none of this had happened."*

Gandalf replied, *"So do all who live to see such times. But that is not for them to decide. All we have to decide is what to do with the time that is given to us."*

Like Frodo, we wish none of this had happened. The sacrifice of these young men has changed forever the lives of most of us here. Hopes, dreams, plans, the framework and circumstances of our world, changed. We have all lost something. Part of us is missing.

C.S. Lewis suffered the loss of his wife slowly

through cancer. After the experience, he wrote the book *A Grief Observed* in his effort to help others get through the pain which is caused by loss. The book begins with the words, *"No one ever told me that grief felt so like fear."*

Any major change forced upon us has the effect of fear. The Greek word for change is "crisis". The loss of a loved one, whether slowly or suddenly, forces us to realize that we are ultimately not in control of life, which begs the question, "Just how much control do we have?" And it prompts the fear that we have no control at all.

Few people realize that J.R.R. Tolkien wrote appendices to the Lord of the Rings trilogy that explained a few things and tied up loose ends. One such end foreshadowed in the trilogy was the death of Aragorn, the king. As he was dying, Aragorn said, *"In sorrow we must go, but not in despair. Behold! We are not bound forever to the circles of the world, and beyond them is more than memory. Farewell!"*

The first light of hope we receive is the realization that these, our comrades are not forever taken from us, but moved on into the caring hands of God. And in the time intervening we must decide what to do with the time we have remaining. Since these young men were part of us, our actions in their absence are all the more significant.

In A Grief Observed, C.S. Lewis says, *"I thought I could describe a state; make a map of sorrow. Sorrow, however, turns out to be not a state but a process."*

Many have studied and much has been taught about the process of sorrow. One perspective is illustrated in the 1998 Universal Pictures movie Meet Joe Black where the character, William Parish, learns at the beginning of the movie he is about to die. During the course of the movie he discovers what is really important and enduring. In his last words to his daughter, Susan, he says, *"I want you to know how much I love you. That you've given a meaning to my life that I had no right to expect, and that no one can ever take from me."*

The ability to love is a gift from God that helps heal the pain and fear. Our most valuable possessions throughout life are the relationships we develop with those we love. The love we share somehow transcends time, distance, and even death.

Elizabeth Barrett Browning wrote a sonnet to her husband which is now a famous love poem which begins with the words, *"How do I love thee? Let me count the ways. I love thee to the depth and breadth and height my soul can reach, when feeling out of sight for the ends of being and ideal grace."* Just before Elizabeth died, her husband, Robert, asked her, *"How do you feel?"* She replied, *"Beautiful."*

The evidence of the gratitude of a thankful and admiring nation is all around us. Most will never understand the full cost of freedom born by those of us left behind. But the love that transcends time in the hands of the God that cares for us will, in time, bring the healing we so desperately need.

For I know the thoughts that I think toward you, saith the Lord, thoughts of peace, and not of evil, to give you an expected end.

□

VII. In the Darkest Times God is with Us and Will Not Fail Us

I will lift up mine eyes unto the hills, from whence cometh my help. My help cometh from the Lord, which made heaven and earth. He will not suffer thy foot to be moved: he that keepeth thee will not slumber. Behold, he that keepeth Israel shall neither slumber nor sleep. The Lord is thy keeper: the Lord is thy shade upon thy right hand. The sun shall not smite thee by day, nor the moon by night. The Lord shall preserve thee from all evil: he shall preserve thy soul. The Lord shall preserve thy going out and thy coming in from this time forth, and even for evermore.

Eighteen months prior to the start of our present conflict, President Bush said, *"The advance of human freedom - the great achievement of our time, and the great hope of every time - now depends on us. Our nation - this generation - will lift a dark threat of violence from our people and our future. We will rally the world to this cause by our efforts, by our courage. We will not tire, we will not falter, and we will not fail."*

Here in America, we take for granted the great strides we have made over the past decades to ensure peace and justice within our borders. Advances in communication, cooperation, policy, and technology have made it nearly impossible for a criminal to get away with a crime. It is to our benefit, and only right, that we share our knowledge and bring it to bear on criminals who operate worldwide. The most visible part of that knowledge is enforcement, which, outside of our borders, falls mainly to American soldiers, sailors, airmen, and marines.

Franklin D. Roosevelt aptly described the character

of the American warrior when he said, *"The creed of our democracy is that liberty is acquired and kept by men and women who are strong and self-reliant, and possessed of such wisdom as God gives mankind - men and women who are just, and understanding, and generous to others - men and women who are capable of disciplining themselves: for they are the rulers and they must rule themselves."*

The warriors we honor today have taken their place forever among the most noble, those who have shed their blood for the freedom of others. We owe them a debt that can never be repaid.

This struggle we as a nation are engaged in is not new. On Friday, the 14th of June 1985 just after taking off from Athens, Greece, Trans World Airlines Captain John Testrake was confronted by two Lebanese Shiites carrying a pistol and grenades. That is how the hijacking of TWA flight 847 to Rome began. The civilized world was introduced to the epitome of evil as it watched an American Navy diver shot in cold blood and dumped on the tarmac at the Beirut airport. Over the course of 17 days, Captain Testrake was held prisoner aboard the plane, flying his captors back and forth across the Mediterranean.

Yet throughout our struggle, and even before we realized, God has been faithful. Years after the experience, Captain Testrake was asked how being hijacked had impacted his life. He answered, *"I knew the presence and the power of God unlike any other time in my life. I felt His presence in the cockpit."* He also related that during the ordeal he was allowed to read his Bible. Deuteronomy 31:6 caught his attention and encouraged him. *"Be strong and of a good courage, fear not, nor be afraid of them: for the Lord thy God, he it is that doth go with thee; he will not fail thee, nor forsake thee."* After being released he was flown by C-141 to the US Air Force hospital in Wiesbaden, Germany and reunited with his wife. Once in his room she was anxious to share with him the verse of scripture that helped her get through the ordeal. Deuteronomy 31:6, *"Be strong and of a good courage, fear not, nor be afraid of them: for the Lord thy God, he it is that doth go with thee; he will not fail thee, nor forsake thee."* They had discovered the same verse at the same time though they were thousands of miles apart. You can read Captain Testrake's story in his book, Triumph Over Terror.

Let's look at that verse a minute. Have no fear because God is with you; be brave; be strong. It's easy to demonstrate every virtue when things are going great. It's only during the tough times that it's hard to be kind, hard to be patient. It's in the times of loss and pain that fear creeps in. We forget that God loves us. We forget that He is God and He's on our side.

John F. Kennedy said, *"We should not let our fears hold us back from pursuing our hopes."* He realized that fear, the strongest of all emotions, can be debilitating. It can throw us off track. It can blind us to the future by drawing a gloomy curtain around our present circumstances.

That is not to say that our circumstances are never disheartening. The loss of these, our comrades, is a painful wound that we all share.

Jacques Cousteau, the French Naval officer most famous for his deep sea exploration, said, *"If we were logical, the future would be bleak indeed. But we are more than logical. We are human beings, and we have faith and we have hope, and we can work."*

From the beginning of time man has realized the transcendence that sets us apart from everything else; a quality about us that makes us more than what we are; a part of us almost impossible to describe or fully understand that exceeds life. It is there that we truly connect with one another. It is there that we connect with God.

William James, an American pioneer in the field of psychology and philosophy, said, *"Your hopes, dreams and aspirations are legitimate. They are trying to take you airborne, above the clouds, above the storms, if you only let them."*

As the Nazi's were extending their control over Europe, just a few miles west of Amsterdam on Holland's northern coast, a watch repairman and his family were helping Jewish refugees escape. They had a secret room constructed at the back of a closet to hide the refugees from the Nazi's. One day, an informant caused the entire family to be arrested. Corrie ten Boom, along with her sister Betsie, was sent to Scheveningen prison in Holland, then to the concentration camp at Ravensbruck, Germany. Corrie watched as her sister received a fatal beating from one of the guards. Corrie was released after three months due to a clerical error. One week later, all the women her age at Ravensbruck were executed. Her work in the Dutch underground earned her international acclaim, but her faith, her hope, and her trust in God during unbearable circumstances gave her an inner strength and a peace inside that most people never experience.

This morning we honor John Doe, Jim Doe, and Matt Doe. The pride we hold for them will remain in our hearts forever. And as for tomorrow, Corrie ten Boom said, *"Never be afraid to trust an unknown future to a known God."*

VIII. Soldier's Death Shows that what is Good in America is Not Lost

The Lord is my shepherd; I shall not want. He maketh me to lie down in green pastures; He leadeth me beside the still waters. He restoreth my soul: he leadeth me in the paths of righteousness for his name's sake. Yea, though I walk through the valley of the shadow of death, I will fear no evil: for thou art with me; thy rod and thy staff they comfort me. Thou preparest a table before me in the presence of mine enemies: thou anointest my head with oil; my cup runneth over. Surely goodness and mercy shall follow me all the days of my life: and I will dwell in the house of the Lord for ever.

Six years ago a group of 19 young men, motivated by hate and driven by a hostile self-serving ideology, traumatically murdered unsuspecting Americans in a coordinated surprise attack on our own soil. President Bush last week said that we, as a nation, were brought face to face with evil.

We drew together as a nation feeling outrage of a magnitude that had not been felt here in 60 years. Overnight we gained a new national focus. Everything we are about took on a new significance.

Benjamin Cheever recently wrote a book about his experiences growing up in the sixties. Looking back over time he observed how traditions and discipline erode from generation to generation. He commented, *"We weren't nearly as frightened by our parents as they were frightened by theirs. The generation that we've raised is not afraid at all. Or not of us."* It looked like the values in America were slipping away.

Prior to 9-11, it seemed that one of those old time values, patriotism, was a thing of the past. Just when we were getting used to generation "X", generation "Y" began rewriting all the rules. The military was having problems meeting annual recruiting goals. Money was successfully taking center stage as the rise and fall of the DOW Jones index had been at the heart of national attention for some time. The many military missions involving American soldiers in various places around the globe hardly made the news. Heroes were the stuff comic books were made of.

Then the unthinkable happened. Probably everyone in this room can remember where they were, what they were doing, and the thoughts running through their minds as they watched the horror unfold before their eyes. And then the unexpected happened. We, as Americans, put aside our political differences. We collectively discovered that patriotism is more than saying the pledge of allegiance or singing the national anthem occasionally. And patriotism is not dead.

All across America, young men answered an implicit call. Some out of a sense of national pride, some filled with indignation, and some with a sense of duty, joined the military and looked forward to the fight. Tennis superstar, Arthur Ashe once said, *"True heroism is remarkably sober, very un-dramatic. It is not the urge to surpass all others at whatever cost, but the urge to serve others, at whatever cost."* We rediscovered heroes. They were among us all the while.

Though we live in a changing world, some things never change. Old values are sometimes forgotten but never diminished in our heart. The really important things, those most valuable are always there for our rediscovery, but more often than not, something has to happen to jolt us out of our comfort zone for us to get a good perspective and find them.

The United States census bureau defines a family as, *"Two or more persons related by birth, marriage, or adoption, who reside together."* But we have a different perspective; especially Army brats growing up on the move, living all over the world. Army families have the Army for their family.

Every Army brat has to learn to make friends quickly and get used to saying good-bye. Some relationships will pick up again sometime in the future, but no one knows for sure if or when that will happen.

Many years ago, the Fort Leonard Wood Protestant Women of the Chapel gave a needlepoint picture as a farewell gift with the caption, *"Home is where the Army sends you."* And many of us here this morning know the truth in that saying. We here are a family in a very special sense of the word. We understand and appreciate each other in a way an outsider can't understand.

We share a sorrow this morning for these three young men. Not only because they have shown us that what is good in America is not lost or forgotten. Not only because they are heroes, but because in a very real sense they are family. It is our brothers we honor here this morning, and our loss is immense; our souls are heavy.

There is one. One who stays closer than a brother. One who knows pain and understands how to comfort. One who protects us in our darkest hours. One who brings peace. He is always there, even when we forget. His door is always open; He's never too busy to take care of us. He never lacks for mercy or love, even when it looks like there is none to be found. No matter how far we go or how busy we get, He is the Lord, my shepherd.

☐

IX. A True Hero Does what has to Be Done

In the year that king Uzziah died I saw also the Lord sitting upon a throne, high and lifted up, and his train filled the temple. Above it stood the seraphim: each one had six wings; with twain he covered his face, and with twain he covered his feet, and with twain he did fly. And one cried unto another, and said, Holy, holy, holy, is the Lord of hosts: the whole earth is full of his glory. And the posts of the door moved at the voice of him that cried, and the house was filled with smoke. Then said I, Woe is me! For I am undone; because I am a man of unclean lips, and I dwell in the midst of a people of unclean lips: for mine eyes have seen the King, the Lord of hosts. Then flew one of the seraphims unto me, having a live coal in his hand, which he had taken with the tongs from off the altar: And he laid it upon my mouth, and said, lo, this hath touched thy lips; and thine iniquity is taken away, and thy sin purged. Also I heard the voice of the Lord, saying, whom shall I send, and who will go for us? Then said I, Here am I; send me.

This morning we have gathered to remember and honor these young heroes of the republic. You have just been given a peek into their lives. I would like to take a glimpse at the unseen, an aspect of their character, part of why we call them heroes.

We all experience the world, and usually we take things for granted. For the most part, people go with the flow and try not to venture out of their comfort zone. It's the American way right? *"Life, liberty, and the pursuit of happiness!"*

A hero stands out from the crowd. He has integrity

of the kind that does the right thing when no one is looking. He sees a need and is not afraid to meet it. George Bernard Shaw said, *"Liberty means responsibility. That is why most men dread it."* The hero hears the call and answers.

Just a couple of days ago I saw and elderly couple with their faces beaming walk up to a soldier in uniform and thank him for serving our nation. America knows. Not many young men are willing to lay their lives on the line to right the wrongs and defend the defenseless. And as noble a calling as it is, they don't do it for the glory.

In his play Twelfth Night, William Shakespeare wrote, *"Be not afraid of greatness: some men are born great, some achieve greatness and some have greatness thrust upon them."* A hero achieves greatness through the integrity of his character. When greatness is thrust upon him, he does not shirk it away or pass it off to someone else. Like the name plate on President Truman's desk which proclaimed, *"The Buck Stops Here,"* he soberly accepts the responsibility.

Doing what's right is often neither easy nor comfortable. Any soldier can tell you that a soldier's life is rough and filled with self-sacrifice on many levels. Perhaps Mark Twain had a soldier in mind when he penned the words, *"Make it a point to do something every day that you don't want to do. This is the golden rule for acquiring the habit of doing your duty without pain."*

Most folks think of duty explicitly; only what the law and the boss demand. Nobel Peace Prize laureate the Dalai Lama, having been honored by President Bush and the United States Congress, once described duty implicitly when he said, *"I believe that to meet the challenges of our times, human beings will have to develop a greater sense of universal responsibility. Each of us must learn to work not just for oneself, one's own family or nation, but for the benefit of all humankind.*

Universal responsibility is the key to human survival. It is the best foundation for world peace."

Heroes, whether consciously or not, grasp the concept of universal responsibility. They understand deep inside what Luke 12:48 meant by, *"For unto whomsoever much is given, of him shall be much required: and to whom men have committed much, of him they will ask the more."*

But don't be mistaken. There is a reward in paying the price. For the hero is not afraid to live life and has a full life as a reward. Theodore Roosevelt said, *"It is not the critic who counts, not the man who points out how the strong man stumbled, or where the doer of deeds could have done better. The credit belongs to the man who is actually in the arena, whose face is marred by dust and sweat and blood, who strives valiantly, who errs and comes short again and again, who knows the great enthusiasms, the great devotions, and spends himself in a worthy cause, who at best knows achievement and who at the worst if he fails at least fails while daring greatly so that his place shall never be with those cold and timid souls who know neither victory nor defeat."* The hero doesn't sit on the sidelines of life but makes life happen. Ultimately he will also get the credit no matter what the pundits say or think.

The hero takes stock of who he is and what he has. His confidence outweighs his fears. He is compelled by an inner prompting: If not me, who?

In the 20th Century Fox movie, Live Free or Die Hard, Justin Long plays computer programmer Matt Farrell, targeted for assassination by a ruthless group of domestic terrorists. Shortly after a dramatic rescue by New York City cop John McClane, played by Bruce Willis, the two have this interchange:

McCLANE: *Hey...how come you ain't yapping?*
MATT: *'Cause I'm scared to death. I'm not like you; All heroic and stuff.*

McCLANE: *I ain't like that at all.*

MATT: *Actually dude...you totally are.*

McCLANE: *I don't want to hear it. I got called that once. Long time ago, and even then I wasn't trying to be.*

MATT: *What did you do?*

McCLANE: *Doesn't matter. They slapped me on the back and I got my fifteen minutes. But you know what? It ain't that great. It gets inside your head and starts breaking the furniture. Cost me a marriage. My kids don't talk to me. I don't want to be that guy again.*

MATT: *But you are.*

McCLANE: *I'm just as scared as you and I'm not sure what in the world we're doing.*

MATT: *Then why are we doing it?*

McCLANE: *Because there isn't anybody else. Believe me if there was, I'd let 'em, but there isn't...so it's got to be us.*

MATT: *And that's what makes you that guy.*

The true hero sees the situation, takes stock of his own abilities and steps up to the challenge. He doesn't look for someone else to do what has to be done but gets involved personally, doing the right thing in spite of fear and without regard for his own need because he must.

This morning we honor Sergeant John Doe, Corporal Jim Doe, and Specialist Matt Doe. Three young men who fit the description: Hero. They fulfilled their higher calling and thereby became better men, and made the world a little better as well.

☐

X. Death Brings Life into Focus

The Lord is my light and my salvation; whom shall I fear? The Lord is the strength of my life; of whom shall I be afraid? When the wicked, even mine enemies and my foes, came upon me to eat up my flesh, they stumbled and fell. Though a host should encamp against me, my heart shall not fear: though war should rise against me, in this will I be confident.

There was a man in the land of Uz named Job who is described in the beginning of the book of Job as perfect, upright, God-fearing, and shunning evil. He was one of the richest men in his time and well respected. He owned thousands of sheep, camels, oxen, and donkeys. He was also the father of 10 children.

Some of you may know the story. In a single day he was attacked by two separate enemies and the victim of two natural disasters. He lost everything including his ten children. Shortly afterward he lost his health so that he was in immense pain. When Job's three friends came to check on him, they saw how much pain he was in, and so they sat down beside him and remained silent for an entire week.

Some say the book of Job, estimated to be around 6,000 years old, was written to answer the question of why bad things happen to good people. It's no secret, and every major religion has attempted to answer that question. It doesn't make sense. It's not logical with what we believe about God.

Job's faith was tested. He cursed the day he was born. Even his wife encouraged him to curse God; die, and get it over with. I'm assuming she did so out of her love for him. Job, in the meantime, questioned everything he knew about God.

Losing the people that are most precious to you has a

way of bringing life into focus. Things that were once very important lose their significance. In the second sequel to the Disney movie, Pirates of the Caribbean, Elizabeth meets her father, the governor, on his way to the other side. He says to her, *"Elizabeth, I think I'm dead, there was something about a chest and a heart; seems a silly thing to die for now."*

C.S. Lewis, extensive author, theologian, and college professor, most famous today for his Chronicles of Narnia, married an American woman named Joy. They weren't married that long when she was diagnosed with cancer and died. After the ordeal he said, *"You never know how much you really believe anything until its truth or falsehood becomes a matter of life and death to you."*

The death of private Doe raises more questions than answers. A bright, ambitious, carefree young man snatched away in the prime of his youth; a loss for us all, but a deep loss to those who were closest to him.

In our human psyche we naturally try to explain our losses to lessen their impact. But loss always brings questions and always brings grief.

I could not stand before you today if I thought the story ended there. For I know in my heart there is a loving God who is in the business of healing and restoration. On the reverse side of your bulletin you will find the words, *"Yea, though I walk through the valley of the shadow of death, I will fear no evil: for thou art with me."*

Grief is a process of healing. Grief takes us on a journey from numb and confused to peace. When David wrote the 23rd Psalm he had already experienced grief. He knew from experience that God is faithful, that's why he had no fear. The opposite of fear is faith.

Job questioned everything he knew about God. His friends tried to convince him that his predicament was entirely his fault.

"Job, you had to have done something; God doesn't work

like that."

Finally, in the 42nd chapter, way toward the end of the book, God answered Job. In his answer God reminded Job of his works; the strength and complexity of creation. God reminded him of His power. God reminded him of His righteousness and His love.

And Job said something incredibly interesting considering how he was characterized at the beginning of the book. He said to God, *"I see you for the first time."*

Another consequence of grief is it enables us to draw closer to God than ever before. It allows Him to meet our needs in a way we never experienced before. And quite possibly, like Job, to see God for the first time.

We grieve over the loss of our comrade John Doe, but we look with faith to a God of comfort who has promised that He will be with us in the darkest times, and as we refocus our lives on what truly matters, He will bring about a bright ending.

XI. The Significance of Life

He that dwelleth in the secret place of the most High shall abide under the shadow of the Almighty. I will say of the LORD, He is my refuge and my fortress: my God; in him will I trust. Surely he shall deliver thee from the snare of the fowler, and from the noisome pestilence. He shall cover thee with his feathers, and under his wings shalt thou trust: his truth shall be thy shield and buckler.

We are here this morning to remember and honor PFC Matt Doe, a beloved son, brother, friend and comrade suddenly taken, a mere twenty years old. He died at home while on his mid tour rest break from Iraq. Nothing was happening out of the ordinary, there was no warning of the tragedy that struck. In a single instant countless lives were changed. Matt's life was cut too short, and as I reflected on the devastation, the loss, the feelings of family and friends, I contemplated life's meaning.

Isn't life too short for us all? Anthony Hopkins' character in the 1998 Universal Pictures movie Meet Joe Black, knowing he's about to die says, *"Sixty years, don't they go by in a blink."*

Mark Twain once said, *"Death, the only immortal who treats us all alike, whose pity and whose peace and whose refuge are for all - the soiled and the pure, the rich and the poor, the loved and the unloved."*

It is only at times like these when the certainty of death enters our minds. We usually go about our everyday affairs as if life will go on forever. We struggle to get ahead. We work to be secure. We fight to be important and strive to be comfortable. In such a frame of mind we waste moments which only become precious in hindsight.

Abbott Eliot Kittredge put it like this: *"My friend, there will come one day to you a Messenger, whom you cannot treat with contempt. He will say, 'Come with me;' and all your pleas of business cares and earthly loves will be of no avail. When his cold hand touches yours, the key of the counting-room will drop forever, and he will lead you away from all your investments, your speculations, your bank-notes and real estate, and with him you will pass into eternity, up to the bar of God. You will not be too busy to die."*

And I wonder, am I too busy to live. In the light of death, what is worth living for? Is it only about me? Surely the ultimate value in life is bigger than my petty day to day concerns, yet how much effort do I put into my own plans; how often do I insist on my own way.

Leo Buscaglia said that, *"Ancient Egyptians believed that upon death they would be asked two questions and their answers would determine whether they could continue their journey in the afterlife. The first question was, 'Did you bring joy?' The second was, 'Did you find joy?'"*

He doesn't go on to explain what the correct answers are, but the two questions get to the heart of the meaning of life.

Many folks, maybe most folks, believe life is fulfilled through experience, like the old beer commercial which proclaimed you only go around once so grab all the gusto you can get. Eleanor Roosevelt said, *"The purpose of life, after all, is to live it, to taste experience to the utmost, to reach out eagerly and without fear for newer and richer experiences."*

Other folks believe life is fulfilled by serving others. That can mean many different things because others have intricate and varied needs. Sometimes, though, it's as simple as taking time to be patient or making the effort to be kind to someone. Mark Twain suggested that when he said, *"Let us endeavor so to live that, when we come to die, even the undertaker will be sorry."*

Live for self or live for others. The two opposite pursuits are brought into a stark contrast in the city of Sodom in ancient Israel. Very few people are aware of the sin Sodom was guilty of. According to Ezekiel 16, the sin of Sodom was they thought they were better than everyone else; they had plenty of free time, lots of food, and they ignored the needy people around them. Their selfish, callous attitude led them down the path to destruction.

Think about those two opposite pursuits. Think about who is held in higher esteem. Isn't it true that Matt's death is all the more tragic because he was a soldier, serving his country, putting his life on the line in a hostile country far from home? So, even at his tender age, his life had significant meaning. He had some of the newer richer experiences, but as a benefit of his heart for service which gave an even richer experience.

Today, death is fresh in our minds. It should also serve as a reminder that the significance of life is living with other people in mind. It's not easy. Our nature pursues self-comfort. Thinking of others first is sincere self-sacrifice, and at the heart of self-sacrifice is trust in God.

There is tremendous comfort when things are not going your way to stop fighting what is, and realize that God is in control, and He knows what He's doing. He's brought us along this far with no indication that He will ever quit on us.

David said in the Psalms, *"What time I am afraid, I will trust in thee. In God I will praise his word, in God I have put my trust; I will not fear what flesh can do unto me."*

ABOUT THE AUTHOR

Richard Sones grew up as the eldest son of an Army Signal Corps officer and, as such, lived all over the world. Moving frequently, he attended army chapels and benefitted by learning under the guidance of chaplains from many different Christian denominations. After earning a Master's degree in Divinity, he was ordained as the pastor of a small, 150 year old church in rural Virginia.

As an advantage of growing up in the military and serving as an army chaplain himself, Richard took the opportunities to explore first hand many of the historical sites of the church.

Now retired from the army after serving nearly 28 years, he continues in ministry as the chaplain of a major hospital in El Paso, Texas where he lives with his wife of 35 years. His four children are grown and on their own adventures in life.

Richard enjoys teaching as much as any aspect of ministry. He has a heart and knack for taking complicated themes and making them easy to understand. Due largely to the leadership training he received over the course of his military career, he is adept at putting things in perspective, cutting through the fluff, and getting to the meat of a topic.

www.ingramcontent.com/pod-product-compliance
Lightning Source LLC
Chambersburg PA
CBHW070812290526
45795CB00002B/697